Below the misty blue mountain was a wild, dark forest and by the wild, dark forest was a village.

The village had a stream and a duck pond and an old red apple tree and it was home to **Aladdin** and his fairytale friends.

Aladdin and his family had just moved to the village.

Keep Trying,

SUE NICHOLSON
Illustrated by LAURA BRENLLA

Once Upon A Time...

...there was a misty blue mountain.

Quarto is the authority on a wide range of topics.

Quarto educates, entertains and enriches the lives of our readers—enthusiasts and lovers of hands-on living.

www.quartoknows.com

Author: Sue Nicholson
Illustrator: Laura Brenlla
Designer: Victoria Kimonidou
Editor: Emily Pither

First Published in 2019 by QED Publishing, an imprint of The Quarto Group.
The Old Brewery, 6 Blundell Street, London N7 9BH, United Kingdom.
T (0)20 7700 6700 F (0)20 7700 8066
www.QuartoKnows.com

A catalogue record for this book is available from the British Library.

ISBN 978-0-7112-4469-6

Manufactured in Shenzhen, China PP072019

9 8 7 6 5 4 3 2 1

MIX
Paper from
responsible sources
FSC® C001701

"We're having an ice-skating party next weekend,"
Goldilocks told Aladdin on his first day at school.
"Would you like to come?"

"Yes, please!"
said Aladdin.

The only problem was, Aladdin didn't know
how to ice-skate. He didn't even have any skates.

Aladdin told his parents about the ice-skating party when he got home.

"That sounds like fun," said his mother, "but how will you learn in time?"

"We can't buy you any skates for a while," added his father.

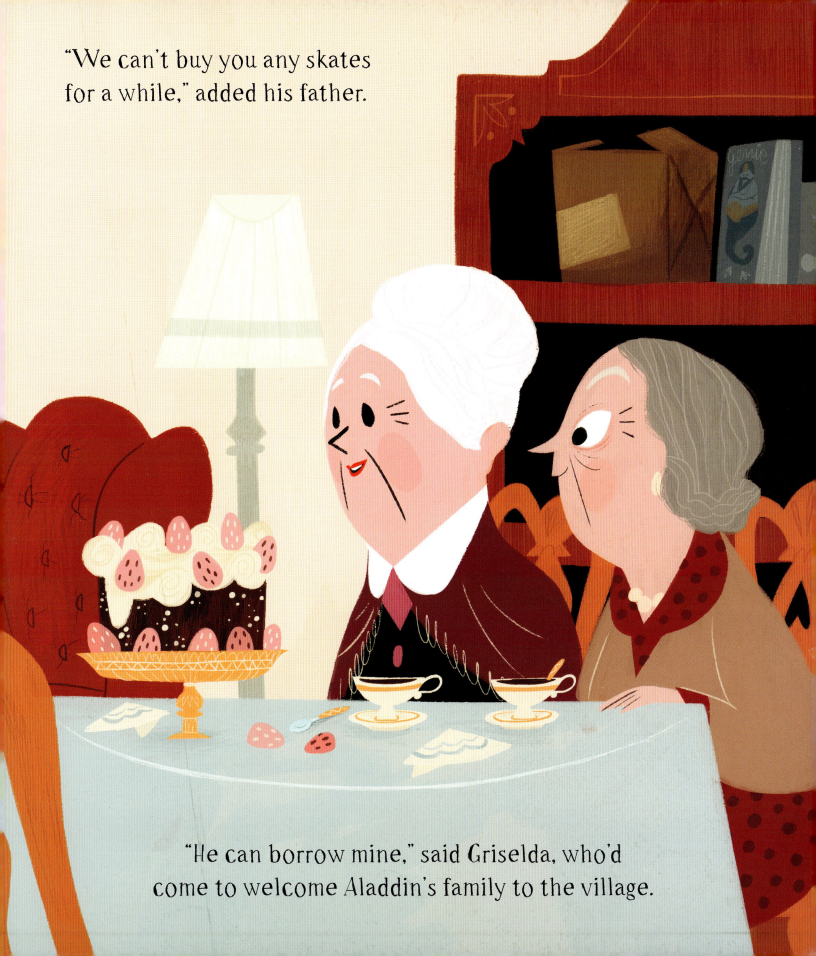

"He can borrow mine," said Griselda, who'd come to welcome Aladdin's family to the village.

Griselda's skates fitted perfectly, but ice-skating was much harder than it looked...

Wobble...

...wobble...

Aladdin's new friends came to skate on the pond.

"Try taking little steps on the ice like this," Cinderella showed him.

"Push off with your feet and glide," said Goldilocks.

"Hold out your arms for balance," said Jack, "and don't look down!"

Aladdin kept trying but...

... wobble...

...wobble...

... wobble...

... BUMP!

... wobble...

... wobble...

... wobble...

... BUMP!

"You just need to keep practising," called Goldilocks.

"It took me ages to learn," said Jack.

But Aladdin was fed up. He sat on the bank watching his friends. They made it look so easy as they sped across the ice.

"It's too hard. I'll never be able to do it - especially in these old skates," thought Aladdin.

That night, Aladdin's father read Aladdin a story about a boy who finds an old magic lamp. When he rubs it, a genie appears and grants him three wishes.

"If only I had three wishes," sighed Aladdin. "I'd wish I could skate. I'd wish I had my own ice-skates. And I'd wish the pond stays frozen for the party."

Aladdin's father smiled. "Well, we don't have a magic lamp, so we can only hope the pond stays frozen, and you're lucky Griselda lent you her skates. As for your other wish – well, that's up to you!"

Aladdin knew his father was right.
If he wanted to learn to skate, he mustn't give up.
He raced to the pond the next day after school.

"Hello!" called Griselda. Aladdin
gasped as she did a graceful spin.

"I'm glad you've come back to try again!" called Griselda. "Remember the tips your friends gave you. You'll be skating in no time!"

Aladdin borrowed Griselda's skates again. This time, he was determined.

He started with little steps, just as Cinderella had suggested...

... BUMP!

Next, he tried pushing off with his feet and gliding...

... BUMP!

He got back up and tried again,
holding out his arms and looking ahead...

... until he was doing it. **He was skating!**

Aladdin ran home to tell his family. There was a surprise waiting for him - a brand new pair of skates.

"We bought them when we were sure you weren't going to give up," his father told him.

"Thank you!" cried Aladdin. "Only I may not be able to skate now after all. Look!" He pointed to the icicles hanging over the window. "They're melting."

Aladdin lay in bed that night, listening to the drip drip drip
of melting ice. He felt sure the ice on the pond must be
melting, too. But the next morning...

...the whole village was covered in snow and the pond was still frozen. It was perfect for the ice-skating party.

"*I'm so glad I kept trying!*" said Aladdin,
as he whizzed across the ice with his friends.

Next Steps

Discussion points

Discuss with the children what the word 'perseverance' means and that sometimes we must try hard at something we might not be able to do straight away. Give the example of riding a bike or learning your times tables. Talk about the importance of not giving up when faced with a challenge. Below are suggestions for discussion points about the story. These will help children with their comprehension skills, as well as developing their understanding of facing a challenge, trying your hardest and not giving up.

- What did Aladdin want to achieve?
  - Have you ever wanted to achieve something?
- Aladdin kept trying and he didn't give up. Why do you think he nearly gave up? Why do you think he found skating difficult? What words does the author use to show us that it was challenging for Aladdin when he was trying to skate?
  - What ways do you think that you can show perseverance?
- How was Griselda helpful?
  - Has anyone ever helped you achieve something you wanted to try or do?
- What did Aladdin wish for?
  - What would you wish for if you had three wishes?
- Think about the ending of the story. Why was it happy for everyone?

Reach for the stars

Give each child a large outline of a star on yellow paper and ask them to cut it out. Ask them to write down a dream, goal or activity that they would like to try on the star. Then give each child a smaller piece of white paper and ask them to draw a picture of themselves. Give each child a large narrow piece of black sugar paper and ask them to glue their star to the top of the paper and to blue tack their picture at the bottom of the paper. Encourage them to draw smaller stars to decorate their picture. These could be put up on the wall and the children can then move their picture up towards their goal as they keep trying to achieve it. You could even do one yourself to be a good role model.